The 1st Clean Sex
Quote and Joke Book

Dr. Allen Unruh

Xulon
PRESS

Copyright © 2004 by Abstinence Clearinghouse
Dr. Allen Unruh
Allen Unruh D.C.
600 N. Western Ave.
Sioux Falls, SD 57104
605-332-1962

The 1st Clean Sex Quote and Joke Book
by Dr. Allen Unruh

Printed in the United States of America

ISBN 1-594676-76-3

www.xulonpress.com

To my wife *Leslee*
and our five children

THE 1ST

CLEAN SEX JOKE BOOK

BY DR. ALLEN UNRUH

I dedicate this book to my wife, Leslee, and our 5 children.

The kids have always consulted with me first on this important topic, that is, when Leslee is out of town, the neighbors are gone, and the dog has run away.

Our oldest when he was a senior said, "Mom, you don't need to give me the hormone talk anymore, I don't have any, you've talked them to death."

I told my daughters' boyfriends that I expect them to treat our daughters with respect, and for backup I own a shotgun and a shovel. I told our daughters to never let a fool kiss you, and never let a kiss fool you.

My wife is passionate about abstinence. She eats, drinks, and sleeps abstinence. Why, just the other night at 3:00

A.M. she sat up in bed and shouted, "Abstinence." I woke up startled and said, "What's happening?" Leslee and I have an agreement: I don't try to run her life and I don't try to run mine and it's worked out very well. She has a philosophy that I can do anything she sets her mind to. Leslee and I vowed to grow old together; we just didn't realize it would be the first year.

To the boys we said, "Flies spread disease – keep yours zipped." Too many men want to sow their wild oats and pray for crop failure in the morning. Loose women usually fall apart. Deep down they're pretty shallow. Our middle son once asked, "How do you know if it's puppy love, Dad?" I said, "Feel your nose, if it's cold and wet it's puppy love, just don't soil the carpet on the way out of the room."

Times have changed:

When I was a kid, I didn't date because I was too shy, about $20.00 too shy. I was so shy I couldn't play tennis with a girl, because I couldn't get myself to say, "Love,-30." In most sports, emotions are crucial, but in tennis, love means nothing at all.

When I was a kid, the only bad thing on TV was the reception – that was kind of snowy. The other day I went to my first X-rated Western – even the wagons weren't covered. When I was a kid, Pot was something you put under the bed so you didn't need to take the trip. The only tanning parlor was the woodshed.

Teaching kids about relationships in the home is crucial. I read about a guy who became a world champion sculpturer and he had no arms. How did he do it? He held a chisel in his mouth, while his wife beat him in the back of the head with a mallet. A woman once told me she married a ventriloquist and discovered he snored on both sides of her at once. She said, "I didn't know it was going to be this bad." One woman said, "I don't really mind PMS, it's the only time of the month I can be myself." But in spite of the difficulties, research has proven that marriage is healthy. Single people die a lot sooner than married people. So if you're looking for a long life, and a slow death, get married.

Sit down on your couch with a cup of green tea full of anti-oxidants and enjoy this book. Sex is the most talked about, sung about, and written about subject in the world, but the paradox is: It's the least understood. That's why I felt compelled to write this book. I got excited just writing it. Hopefully there will be a few pearls of wisdom for everyone on this vital topic.

When it comes to sex before marriage, you need to learn to:

• Purge your urge
• Put your lust in the dust, and your drive in park
• If you indulge, you may bulge
• Pet your dog, not your date, even if your date's a dog
• You must learn that a man cannot live on BED alone, or you will not end up in a halfway house, but an all the way house for girls who went all the way.
• The best oral contraception is the word, "NO!"
• A sperm of the moment decision has ruined many a life.
• One mistake leads to a mother.
"The next time a girl tells you that you can go as far as you want, drive her to Minneapolis." Allen Unruh

A hypocrite is a person who complains about all the sex and violence on his VCR.

THE IMPORTANCE OF A
SENSE OF HUMOR

A merry heart is important to dispel sexual tension and attract the right mate. "A merry heart of doeth good like medicine but a broken spirit drieth up the bones." Proverbs 17:22

Too many think being single is like a disease. Controlling hormones will create some major deficiency syndrome. Men say, "If I don't get rid of this sexual tension, I'm going to die." Well, so far nobody has died due to self-control. But many have died from lack of self-control. One woman was reading the obituaries and said, "Well, he finally died." "Who?" asked her husband. "Charlie Ashford. He said if I didn't marry him he was going to die, and he finally died. It only took him 50 years."

Usually a cold shower will do the trick very rapidly. Actually, you can make it a fun experience by using humor.

Shared laughter is a prescription for any relationship. Relationships and marriage inevitably bring challenges. Crisis, transitions, and difficulties surface, demanding our attention. There's one last element necessary for managing the storms of life, a sense of humor.

Choosing to see the lighter side makes marriage a lot easier. A sense of humor eases tension, gives perspective, joins couples in the intimacy of a shared experience, and often clears the mind and heart, helping couples solve their problems.

It's important to lighten up. Learn to laugh at yourself. See the humor in each situation.

Abortion

1. "I've noticed that 100 percent of the people who are pro abortion have already been born."   Ronald Reagan

2. "I have to march, because my mother didn't have the right to have an abortion."   Maxine Waters, Democrat from California in a speech at a pro-abortion rally in Washington, D.C., printed in the *Washington Times,* May 3, 2004.

Abstinence

1. Did you hear about the 92-year-old virgin who got married? On his wedding night his bride said, "Why don't we go upstairs and make love?" He said, "Listen, I can't do both."

2. I had an aunt who waited so long for her ship to come in that her pier collapsed.

3. Abstinence is one subject you should not practice in moderation.

4. Too many men want to sow their wild oats and then pray for crop failure in the morning.

5. One guy said, "When I asked my girlfriend if she wanted to have sex, she used an oral contraceptive — she said "NO!""

6. With 64 million cases of incurable sexually transmitted diseases, the moral of the story is: "Play now and pay later, or pay now and play later."

7. Q: "When are you getting married?" Older woman: "I'm waiting for Mr. Right."

   A: "Which one, Orville or Wilbur?"

8. Familiarity breeds contempt, but you can't breed without familiarity.

9. Man cannot live on bed alone.

10. Birth control pills are deductible, but only if they don't work.

11. When it comes to sex, one mistake can lead to a mother.

12. Familiarity breeds contempt.

13. Flies spread disease — keep yours zipped.

14. I wish everyone would just go back in the closet.

15. There's something about closets nowadays that are making skeletons nervous.

16. Abstinence until marriage — the one time procrastination is a positive experience.

17. Deep down — loose woman are really shallow.

18. Loose women eventually fall apart.

19. What do promiscuity and insanity have in common? They are people who do the same thing over and over and expect a different result.

20. It's better to be king for a night, than a schmuck for a lifetime.

21. Love conquers everything except poverty and a toothache.

22. Cream doesn't rise to the top. It works its way up. If you want to be the cream of the crop for your future mate, you have to work at it.

23. One young woman said, "I used to be snow white, but then I drifted."

24. Premarital sex doesn't relieve tension; it's just the beginning.

25. It's better to have loved and lost than never lost at all.

26. I'm dating a woman who evidently is not aware of it.

27. Women who miscalculate are called mothers.

28. When I hear people talk about birth control I always remember I was the fifth.

29. Abstinence is the best medicine.

30. Counselor: "Have you ever tried Abstinence?"

    Teenager: "Where do you get those?"

31. Refrain tonight, and that shall lend a kind of easiness to the next abstinence.

32. When in doubt, do without.

33. They read so much of the side effects of promiscuity, they decided to quit reading.

34. Character is what you are in the dark.

35. Men use power to gain sex, women use sex to gain power.

36. The greatest strength and wealth is self control.

37. "A man without self control is like a city broken into and left without walls." Proverbs 25:28

38. Rationalization is the art of gaining self respect through self deception.

39. Man discovered fire 2000 years ago and has been playing with it ever since.

40. "The ideal situation is one man and one wife for life." Wilt Chamberlain (who claimed to have had sex with 1000 women)

41. Our son said, "Mom, you don't need to give me the hormone talk anymore. I don't have any more, you talked them to death."

42. When you think about prom night, prom must stand for promiscuous.

43. Two grade school boys were talking when a cute young girl walked passed them. One boy said to the other, "As soon as I quit hating girls she is the first girl I'm going to quit hating."

44. There's no such thing as free sex — there's always free cheese in a mouse trap.

45. Sex is like fire — a dangerous servant and a fearful master.

46. Love is blind — that's why we will always have hippopotamuses.

47. Dennis Rodman tried to change his name to "orgasm." That's because dumb schmuck was already taken.

48. Passion — Did you hear about the ant that married the elephant? After their first night the elephant died. The ant said, "Just my luck, one night of passion and I have to spend the rest of my life digging a grave."

    MORAL: Millions of young people are digging their own graves from one night of passion.

49. Ever since we got our waterbed we've been drifting apart.

50. Abstinence should be practiced at every conceivable moment prior to marriage.

51. You can't be abstinent in moderation.

52. Too much liberty leads men to slavery. The basis of liberty is moral restraint.

53. "I know how you feel about liberty, but this is your third night out this week." Patrick Henry's wife

ACCOUNTABILITY

The consequences of promiscuity may not be noticed immediately, but they will come as night follows day. It's like the guy who jumped off the Empire State Building and every window he went by he hollered, "I'm all right so far."

ADAM & EVE

1. One day Eve said to Adam, "Do you love me?" He said, "Who else?"

2. Adam said to Eve, "What do you mean you have nothing to wear?"

3. Adam said to Eve one day, "Just remember, there's more ribs where you came from."

4. Adam took his kids to the Garden of Eden and said, "There's where your ma ate us both out of house and home."

5. Adam said to Eve, "I'll wear the plants in this family."

6. Eve made dinner once and Adam said, "You've done it again Eve, you've put my shorts in the salad."

7. God created man in his own image. He put him in a beautiful Garden of Eden. He said, "Replenish the earth and subdue it." So he gave him Albert.

8. When God created woman he put Adam in a deep sleep. The scriptures don't record he ever came out of it.

9. This used to be a man's world. Then Eve arrived.

ADVICE

1. Advising a fool is like beating air with a stick.

2. Any man who has to ask for advice probably isn't married.

3. Start slow and taper off.

4. In closing here's my advice to couples: I want you to lie, cheat, steal and divorce.   Lie in bed together longer than normal at least a few times a week.   Cheat on your diet and take your wife out to dinner more often and spend time together alone.   Steal some time to travel and enjoy each other's company.   And divorce yourself from some of the responsibilities where you are majoring on the minors, and spend it on your relationship.

AGING

1. My wife gave me some Old Spouse for my birthday, so I gave her some Oil of Old Lady for hers.

2. The best cure for wrinkles is Preparation H. The only side effect is when you get tired, your face wants to sit down.

3. This old couple was sitting on rocking chairs on their front porch. Finally the husband said, "Honey, I'd have been a dynamic success if it weren't for all your lousy decisions."

4. Wisdom doesn't always come with old age. Sometimes old age comes all by itself.

5. A guy put up a billboard that read: "Old millionaire wants young woman." The next day he found one. Someone who wanted an older man with a big heart, but she said, "An enlarged heart would be even better."

6. This old baldheaded guy with a big gut is standing at a counter in a motel and this young blonde walks up. He looks at her and says, "Well hellooooo dare, where have you been all my life?" She looked at him and said, "Well, for the first half of it I hadn't been born."

7. The billionaire who married a young blonde model died. After his death she had three days of mourning followed by several months of shopping.

8. This old guy was feeling lousy and went to the doctor who examined him and gave him some advice. A week later the doctor sees this old guy walking down the street with a young blonde under his arm, with a spring in his step and a smile on his face. The doctor walks up and says, "What happened to you Charlie?" He said, "I'm just following your advice doctor." The doctor said, "What's that?" Charlie said, "You said to get a hot mamma and be cheerful." The doctor exclaimed, "No, I said you got a heart murmur and be careful!"

9. The number one group of people with AIDS is senior citizens, according to the latest research. They have government AID, digestive AIDS, and hearing AIDS.

10. Even Dolly Parton's career is sagging.

11. My aunt waited so long for her ship to come in that her Pier collapsed.

12. My grandmother used to sleep with 4 different boyfriends a night; Arthritis, Ben Gay, Charlie Horse, and Will Power.

13. By the time a man has money to burn the fire has gone out.,

14. This 98-year-old man marries a 97-year-old. They said, "Till death do us part or Thursday, whichever comes first." They were registered at the Hill of Rest.

Aging Cont.

15. This couple who had been married 60 years was sitting on rocking chairs on the front porch. The husband says to his wife, "Honey, our marriage has stood the test of time, our relationship is tried and true." She hollered, "What!" He said, "Tried and true." She hollered, "What!" He hollered back, "Tried and true, tried and true." She said, "I'm getting tired of you too."

16. What mother nature giveth, father time taketh away.

17. Youth and beauty fade, character endures forever.

Bathing Suits

1. When they advertise bathing suits half off nowadays, they're not kidding.

2. The mini skirt was the only problem where the end was in sight.

CHARACTER

Strong convictions precede great actions. Abstinence builds character.

CHIVALRY

"Chivalry is the most delicate form of contempt."
Albert Guerard

CHOICE

1. "Your capacity to say no determines your capacity to say yes to greater things." E. Stanley Jones

2. "We make our decisions and then our decisions turn around and make us." R. W. Boreham

3. "Between two evils,choose neither; between two goods,choose both." Tyron Edwards

4. "The doors we open and close every day decide the lives we live." Flora Whitemore

5. To stay out of hot water, keep a cool head.

COMMUNICATION

1. A lady once said to Yogi Bear, "You're looking pretty cool today." He said, "You don't look so hot yourself."

2. A young blonde went to Africa and came home with a native with beads all around him, a bone through his nose, and his face all painted up. She said, "Mom and Dad, I want you to meet my new husband." The father looked him over and said, "Honey, we wanted you to marry a rich doctor."

3. Tell your girlfriend she looks like a fresh breath of spring, not the end of a cold, long, hard winter.

4. "We need four hugs a day for survival. We need 8 hugs a day for maintenance. We need 12 hugs a day for growth." Virginia Satir, family therapist

5. A little common sense would prevent most divorces – and marriages, too.

Condoms

1. Condoms aren't always safe. One guy said he tried one and got hit by a bus.

2. Are we a Christian nation or a condom nation?

3. A mother was scolding her 16-year-old son when she found a condom lying on the floor in the patio. His 6 year-old younger brother was listening in and later asked, "What's a patio?"

4. Are condoms Holy or holey? Are they the Savior of sex or its' destruction?

Conscience

1. "It is an accepted law of ethics that punishment in the Court of Conscience, unlike that in Courts of Law, lessens with each repeated and unrebuked offense." Joseph Auerbach

2. "A disciplined conscience is a man's best friend. It may not be his most amiable, but it is his most faithful monitor." Henry Beecher

29

3. "A reason often makes mistakes, but a conscience never does." John Billings

4. "It is far more important to me to preserve an unblemished conscience than to compass any object however great." William Channing

5. "A man that will enjoy a quiet conscience, will lead a quiet life." Lord Chesterfield

6. He who sacrifices his conscience to ambition burns a picture to obtain the ashes. Chinese Proverb

7. "Conscience is the root of all true courage; if a man would be brave let him obey his conscience." James Clarke

8. "The truth is not so much that man has conscience as that conscience has man." Isaac Dorner

9. "The man who has won millions at the cost of his conscience is a failure." B.C. Forbes

10. "A quiet conscience sleeps in thunder." Thomas Fuller

11. "If your conscience won't stop you, pray for cold feet." Elmer Letterman

12. "Conscience is the inner voice that warns us that someone may be looking." H. L. Mencken

13. "The foundation of the true joy is in the conscience." Seneca

14. "Conscience is God's presence in man." Emanuel Swedenborg

15. "Conscience is that which hurts when everything else feels good." George Vavoulis

16. "Labor to keep alive that little spark of celestial fire called conscience." George Washington

17. "If a dog will not come to you after he has looked you in the face, you ought to go home and examine your conscience." Woodrow Wilson

CONSCIENCE CONT.

18. Conscience: something that feels terrible when everything else feels wonderful.

19. Conscience is a playback of the still small voice that told you not to do it in the first place.

20. He who has a fight with his conscience and loses, wins.

21. "A man has less conscience when in love than in any other condition."   Schopenhauer

22. Conscience helps, but the fear of getting caught doesn't do any harm either.

23. Living without conscience is like driving a sports car with no brakes.

24. "It is neither safe nor prudent to do anything against the conscience."   Martin Luther

25. Conscience is that still small voice that yells so loud the morning after.

Conscience Cont.

26. "The man who loses his conscience has nothing left that is worth keeping."   Izaak Walton

27. A blush is one thing that can't be counterfeited.

Dating

1. This guy went to the service for a year, so he decided to write his girlfriend everyday to keep the relationship going. She ended up marrying the postman. The moral of the story is you can do everything right and still lose.

2. "How you catch em is how you keep em."

3. When I dated my wife, she once asked me if I danced and it made me really upset. Why? Because we were dancing when she asked me.

4. After we were married, she said, "Waltz a little faster honey, this is a Rumba."

5. A wink takes 1/40th of a second and it's the fastest way known to man to get into trouble.

6. It's statistically proven that the odds of meeting a single guy are 1 in 19. His being good looking are 1 in 393, intelligent and good looking, 1 in 136,040, and the odds are 1 in 1,753,000 that she'd meet him on a good hair day.

7. When I finally married Mr. Right, I just didn't realize his first name was "Always."

8. I wanted to marry her from the first moment I saw the moonlight shining on the barrel of her father's shotgun.

9. My future son-in-law said he believes in abstinence but I told him for backup I owned a shotgun and a shovel.

10. A young man was walking in the park with his girlfriend. All of a sudden he blurted out, "Will you marry me?" She said, "Why yes." He never said a word for 3 hours as they kept walking. Finally she said, "Johnny, aren't you going to say anything?" He said, "I think I already said too much."

DATING CONT.

11. A young blonde wrote her boyfriend a letter: Dear Johnny, I'm sorry I raised my voice at you and told you off. I should have never said what I said. I've had a complete change of heart. Please forgive me. I want you. I need you. I can't live without you. Please come back to me. Love, Mary

    PS. Congratulations on winning the million dollar lottery.

12. "I like a woman with a good head on her shoulders, I hate necks." Steve Martin

13. A man in love is incomplete until he's married. Then he's finished.

14. "Zeek, that new son in law walks around like he's got lead in his britches." Zeek "By George, he has."

15. When we were dating my wife asked me if I danced and I got angry. Why? Because we were dancing when she asked me.

DECISIONS

1. "Nothing seems fixed. Everything is always changing. We seem to have very little control over our emotional life." Sherwood Anderson

2. "There is no fire like passion, there is no snare like folly." Buddha

3. "The advantage of the emotions is that they lead us astray." Oscar Wilde

4. Quick decisions are unsafe decisions.

DISCIPLINE

1. Discipline, once considered "standard household equipment," has fallen on hard times, and in its place permissiveness reigns.

2. He who fiddles around seldom gets to lead the orchestra.

3. The actions of some children today suggest that their parents embarked upon the seas of matrimony without a paddle.

EXERCISE

I bought my wife a rowing machine but she said it wouldn't fit in the tub.

FAMOUS WORDS

1. George Washington: "I cannot tell a lie."

   Franklin Roosevelt: "We have nothing to fear, but fear itself."

   Bill Clinton: "Your place or mine?"

2. Clinton: "I only regret that I have but one wife to give for my country."

FATHERS

There are too many fathers who tie up their hound dogs at night and let their boys run loose.

FREE SEX

Free love is too expensive.

Gifts

1. I asked my wife what she wanted for our anniversary. She said she wouldn't mind lunch at Rivera. So I gave her a sandwich on a Buick.

2. My wife said she wanted to see the world, so I bought her an atlas.

3. My wife finally told me, "If you have to plug it in, I don't want it." So I had to take all her gifts back.

4. I once bought her steel belted radials with monogrammed mud flaps. It never went over.

5. I gave her a fake fur once and she fed me a rubber chicken for supper.

6. I gave her a tool set and a new shovel for her birthday, so she bought me a new washer and dryer for mine.

7. I told my wife it could be worse. One guy bought his wife a cemetery plot for her birthday. Something she could always use. The next year he didn't get her anything. She asked, "Honey, why didn't you get me anything?" He said, "You didn't use what I got you last year."

8. I bought my wife a rowing machine and she said it wouldn't fit in the bathtub.

9. I walked in a jewelry store and asked, "I know diamonds are forever, but do you have anything that would just last a few months?"

10. With today's technology, you can have an alarm clock that tells you that you overslept, you get the scale and it tells you that you're overweight. Your refrigerator tells you that you're out of milk. Your toaster asks you how you want your toast. Everything talks to you but your wife. You bought her all these fancy gadgets and she wanted a diamond ring.

GIFTS CONT.

11. One guy went in a department store and asked the clerk how much Poison perfume was. She said, "That will be $175.00." He squirmed and said, "I need something for a little less money." She said, "We have the half size bottle for $100.00." He said, "That's still a little steep." She said, "We have brand X here for $39.00." He still squirmed and said, "Ma'am, I need something really cheap." She said, "I have just what you want," and she opened a drawer and showed him a mirror.

GUIDANCE

Now that we have perfected guided missiles, the only things left that need guidance are young people.

HEADACHES

Even Solomon said to his thousand wives and concubines, "All right, which one of you doesn't have a headache?"

HEALTH

A 92-year-old man went to the doctor to get a physical. A few days later, the doctor saw the man walking down the street with a gorgeous young lady under his arm. The next day at a follow up visit, the doctor said, "You're really doing great Charlie." The man replied, "Just doing what you said doctor. You said to get a hot mamma ad be cheerful." The doctor said, "I didn't say that. I said you've got a heart murmur and be careful."

INTIMACY

1. To build intimacy, no sex before marriage is more intimate after marriage.

2. A lover without feeling is a paltry mediocrity.

3. "Their bodies were so close together that there was no room for real affection." Stanislaw Lec

4. "I'd rather have one woman 10,000 times than 10,000 women one time." Wilt Chamberlain

5. It's hard to get to know somebody when your lips are always together.

LAW

1. In Maryland a man may not marry his wife's grandmother.

2. Did you hear about the woman who sent out 1,500 perfumed erotic valentines signed, "Guess who?" She's a divorce lawyer.

3. Public kissing is only legal in railroad stations in Italy.

4. In London, it's illegal to kiss a girl on Sunday in public.

5. In Japan all public demonstrations of affection are outlawed. Kissing a girl can result in a jail sentence.

LONELINESS

1. "Lonely people talking to each other can make each other lonelier."   Lillian Hellman

2. "When you're all by yourself, are you in good company?"   Allen Unruh

3. "Night brings our troubles to the light rather than banishes them."   Seneca

4. "People are lonely because they build walls instead of bridges."   Joseph Newton

LOOKS

1. "You'd be surprised how much it costs to look this cheap."   Dolly Parton

2. Nature makes boys and girls lovely to look at so they can be tolerated until they acquire some sense.

LOVE

1. The girl who thinks no man is good enough for her may be right, but more often she is left.

2. One of our greatest learning tasks is how to give and to receive love.

3. Love often intoxicates, marriage always sobers.

4. A fool and her money are soon courted.

5. She took me to the tunnel of love and told me to wait outside.

MARRIAGE

1. "Personally, I know nothing about sex, because I've always been married." Zsa Zsa Gabor

2. A man chases a woman until she catches him.

3. When it comes to marriage, you have to learn to take the bitter with the sour.

4. If one wants to have children, the rhythm method is probably the best, but it's hard to find a band at two in the morning.

5. It got so cold in South Dakota one bachelor almost decided to get married.

6. I had a patient who had fake eyelashes, a face lift, a wig, breast implants, and false teeth, and said she was looking for a REAL man.

7. When my wife and I got married we vowed to grow old together. We just didn't realize it was going to be the first year.

8. A couple wanted to get a divorce after 60 years of marriage. Why? Because they wanted to wait until all the kids died.

9. My wife and I got married early. I think it was 2:00.

10. It has been proven that married life is healthy. Statistics show that single people die sooner than married folks. So, if you're looking for a long life and a slow death, get married.

MARRIAGE CONT.

11. I read about a couple who got a divorce the morning after their wedding. It doesn't make sense. I mean, how bad could breakfast have been?

12. The idea of priests getting married is nothing new. You'd be surprised how many men are fathers on their wedding day.

13. There's nothing I wouldn't do for my wife, and there's nothing she wouldn't do for me. And that's the way it's been. We've done nothing for each other for 20 years.

14. My wife and I never go to bed mad. We haven't slept in weeks.

MEN

1. Why don't men wash clothes? Because they don't have a remote.

2. Why does it take 4 billion sperm and only one egg to make a human? Because they don't ask for directions.

3. Q: Do you know what they call a happy sperm?

   A: It's one with egg all over it's face.

4. One guy, after watching football for 6 hours, could hardly get out of the couch. His wife said, "Is that what they call a tight end?"

5. Did you know that man is in the middle of roMANce?

6. One thing women need to realize is that guys with deep rich, dark tans are usually unemployed.

7. I was born in bed with a lady.

8. I sent my picture to the lonely hearts club and they sent it back and said "We're not that lonely."

9. One man to another leaving for home too late at night:
   Q: "Do you think your wife will hit the ceiling?"
   A: "I suppose so, she's a lousy shot."

10. A man named Jones went to his psychologist to be analyzed, and the counselor immediately began to administer the Rorschach Ink Blot Test. He held up the first blot, which looked something like a fox who's been chasing parked cars. He said, "What do you see?" The patient said, "That's a picture of two people making love." The psychologist raised an eyebrow. He held up the second blot, which resembles a couple of people playing patty-cake, and said, "What does this one look like? The patient said, "It's a picture of two people making love." The therapist began to suspect he was onto something. He held up the third blot just to be sure. Now the third blot looks like two people roasting a large butterfly over a campfire. But the psychologist handed it to the man and asked, "And what do you make of this one?" The patient rolled his eyes and said exasperatedly, "It's a picture of two people making love." The psychologist had heard enough. He said, "Mr. Jones, I believe that you have an obsession with sex." Jones was incensed. He couldn't believe what he was hearing. He said, "Me??? I'm obsessed with sex??? YOU'RE THE ONE WITH ALL THE DIRTY PICTURES."

We've become a nation obsessed with sex.

11. Men marry later and die earlier.

12. Why do men reach their sexual prime at the age of 18 and women at 40?

13. Some women get all excited about nothing and then they marry him.

14. Cheap: One guy wanted to buy his wife some perfume. He asked the clerk who pulled out some "Poison" "How much?" He asked. She said, "$175.00." Too much he said so she pulled out another bottle and said, "This one is $75.00." He said, "Too much." She pulled out a $35.00 bottle and he still said, "Too much, I want something really cheap." So the clerk said, "I have just the thing for you." So she reached in a drawer and showed him a mirror.

15. Six-year-old to her mother: "Where are all the dumb idiots Mommy?" Mother: "They're at home dear. They only come out when your father dies."

MENTAL

1. No wonder my wife lost her mind, she's been giving me a piece of it every day for 20 years.

2. There are more men in mental hospitals than women according to a new study. This settles the old argument about who's driving who crazy.

MODESTY

1. The mini skirt problem was the only one where the end was in sight.

2. When they advertise bikinis half off nowadays, they're not kidding.

3. I went to my first x-rated western recently. Even the wagons weren't covered.

4. What to say to a girl wearing a thong on the beach: "Pardon me ma'am, but your rear end has swallowed up your bathing suit."

Modesty Cont.

5. "Modesty is my best quality." Jack Benny

6. "A woman is closest to being naked when she is well dressed." Coco Chanel

Money

1. How did I meet my wife? I opened my wallet and there she was.

2. When we met, I was in the deposit line and she was in the withdrawal line. It's been that way ever since.

3. I nicknamed my wife "Teddy Roosevelt," because everywhere she goes she hollers, "CHARGE!"

4. My wife will buy anything marked down. Last week she bought an escalator.

5. A fool and her money are soon courted.

6. You can't make a silk purse out of a sow's ear, but many a woman has gotten a mink coat out of an old goat.

MONEY CONT.

7. The most popular labor-saving device is still a husband with money.

8. I'm a little nervous. My wife grabbed a shopping cart at Tiffanys.

MOTHERS-IN-LAW

1. My mother-in-law buried 3 husbands, and 2 of them were just napping.

2. Behind every successful man is a surprised mother-in-law.

3. Did you hear about the cannibal who ate his mother-in-law and she still disagreed with him?

4. Mixed emotions are your mother-in-law going over a cliff in your new Mercedes.

5. It only takes two to make a happy marriage...a woman and her mother.

Neatness

1. My wife is neat. She's so neat, she puts newspapers under the cuckoo clock. She washes the windows on envelopes. I mean, when the Saints go marching in, they better wipe their feet. I got up in the middle of the night to go to the bathroom last night, and when I got back, the bed was made.

2. Of course, it could be worse. A friend of mine said his wife was so sloppy that *Good Housekeeping* canceled her subscription.

Nudists

1. The Supreme Court has ruled that nudists aren't covered by the First Amendment. Of course, they're not covered by anything.

2. Nudists say they join for sunshine and health. If that were true, how come you never see any blind nudists? You'd think you'd see one once in a while.

3. They asked a reporter what made the most pronounced impression on her when she visited the nudist camp. She said, "Those cane bottom chairs."

4. Did you hear about the mosquito that flew into the nudist camp? He surveyed the situation and said, "The opportunities here are so vast, I hardly know where to start."

5. Did you hear about the 2 nudists that broke up because they were seeing too much of each other?

6. This is the age of the "Modest Nudist".

7. "Nudists are fond of saying that when you come right down to it, everyone is alike, and again, that when you come right down to it everyone is different."   Diane Arrus

8. When you join a nudist camp, the first two weeks are the hardest.   You don't know what to do with your hands.

PERSONAL ADS

1. SIGN ON BILLBOARD: "Old millionaire wants young woman." The next day he found one. Someone who wanted an older man with a big heart, but she said an enlarged heart would be even better.

2. FOXY LADY: Sexy, fashion-conscious blue-haired beauty, 80's, slim, 5'4" (used to be 5'6"), searching for sharp-looking, sharp-dressing companion. Matching white shoes and belt a plus.

3. LONG-TERM COMMITMENT: Recent widow who has just buried fourth husband looking for someone to round out a six-unit plot. Dizziness, fainting, shortness of breath not a problem.

4. SERENITY NOW: I am into solitude, long walks, sunrises, the ocean, yoga, and meditation. If you are the silent type, let's get together, take our hearing aids out and enjoy quiet times.

Personal Ads Cont.

5. WINNING SMILE: Active grandmother with original teeth seeking a dedicated flosser to share rare steaks, corn on the cob, and caramel candy.

6. MEMORIES: I can usually remember Monday through Thursday. If you can remember Friday, Saturday, and Sunday, let's put our two heads together.

7. MINT CONDITION: Male, 1932, high mileage, good condition, some hair, many new parts including hip, knee, cornea, valves. Isn't in running condition but walks well.

Politics

1. Politics are starting to give sex a bad name.

2. I was reading that 90% of politicians were not breast-fed. Even their mothers didn't trust them.

3. Too many young people nowadays think running for Congress is a great way to meet girls.

POLITICS CONT.

4. "Too many men have entered politics solely because they are unhappily married." C. Northcore Parkinson

③

PUPPY LOVE

1. My son asked me, "Dad, how do I know if it's puppy love?" My answer was, "Feel your nose. If it's cold and wet, it's puppy love; just don't soil the carpet on your way out of the room."

2. Puppy love leads to a dog's life, but it's real to the puppy.

QUOTES ON LOVE

1. A wise lover values not so much the gift of the lover, as the love of the giver.

2. It is not true that love makes all things easy; it makes us choose what is difficult.

3. The love you give is the love you receive.

4. "The inability to love is the definition of hell." Destovsky

5. What a strange illusion to believe that beauty is goodness.

6. Too many think you need somebody to love while they're looking for someone to love.

7. If you want to catch a trout, don't fish in a herring barrel.

8. The animals most often encountered in the single jungle are pigs, dogs, wolves, skunks, slugs, and snakes.

9. My boyfriend and I broke up. He wanted to get married and I didn't want him to.

10. Too many climb the ladder of promiscuity wrong by wrong.

11. "Sex has now become one of the leading statistics. And current research has proven that statistics are only accurate 68% of the time." Allen Unruh D.C.

12. Success in marriage depends on how well you use three books: the Cookbook, the Good book, and the Checkbook.

13. There is no happiness, there are only moments of happiness.

14. Love is an ocean of emotions completely surrounded by expenses.

15. The sweetest joy, the wildest woe, is love.

16. "O what a heaven is love! O what a hell!"   Thomas Middleton

17. "Love begets love, this torment is my joy." Theodore Roethke

18. What a recreation it is to be in love! It sets the heart aching so delicately, there's no taking a wink of sleep for the pleasure of the pain.

19. When my love swears that she is made of truth, I do believe her, though I know she lies.

20. "In love, assurances are practically an announcement of their opposite." Elias Canetti

21. "Where love is concerned, too much is not enough." Pierre De Beaumarchais

22. "To obtain a woman who loves you, you must treat her as if she didn't." Pierre De Beaumarchais

23. "Paper napkins never return from the laundry, nor love from a trip to the law courts." John Barrymore

24. Love: A temporary insanity curable by marriage.

25. "Adam invented love at first sight, one of the greatest time savers of all time." Allen Unruh

26. "Love is an enigma, inside a mystery, inside a riddle." Allen Unruh

27. "I love you, I need you, I want you, I can't live without you," the husband said.   His wife responded, "I, I, I, that's all you ever say is 'I.'"

28. "Like the measles, love is most dangerous when it comes late in life." Lord Byron

29. "Love means to love that which is unlovable or it is no virtue at all." G. K. Chesterton

30. "Many a man has fallen in love with a woman in light so dim he would not have chosen a suit by it." Maurice Chevalier

31. "Every time we hold our tongue instead of returning the sharp retort, show patience with another's faults, show a little more love and kindness, we are helping to stock-pile more of these peace-bringing qualities in the world instead of armaments for war."   Constance Foster

32. How does a porcupine make love?   Very carefully.

33. "The more you love, the more you can love - and the more intensely you love.   Nor is there any limit on how many you can love.   If a person had time enough, he could love all that majority who are decent and just."   Robert Heinlein

34. "Love is what's left of a relationship after all the selfishness has been removed."   Cullen Hightower

35. "Beloved, let us love one another, for love is of God. Everyone that loveth is born of God and knows God. He that loves not knows not God, for God is love."   1 John 4:7-8

36. "A new commandment I give unto you, that ye love one another; as I have loved you, that ye also love one another." John 13:34

37. "Love at first sight is easy to understand. It's when two people have been looking at each other for years that it becomes a miracle."   Sam Levenson

38. "There is no way under the sun of making a man worthy of love, except by loving him." Thomas Merton

39. "To live without loving is not really to live." Moliere

40. "The quarrels of lovers are like summer storms. Everything is more beautiful when they have passed." Suzanne Necker

41. "Those who love deeply never grow old; they may die of old age, but they die young." A.W. Piner2

42. "He whom love touches not walks in darkness." Plato

43. "There is only one kind of love, but there are one thousand imitations." Franquis De La Rochefoucauld

44. "There is no remedy for love but to love more." Henry David Thoreau

45. "The language of love is spoken with a look, a touch, a sigh, a kiss, and sometimes a word." Frank Tyger

QUOTES ON LOVE CONT.

46. "The emotion, the ecstasy of love, we all want, but God spare us the responsibility." Jessamyn West

47. "What we can do for another is the test of power. What we can suffer for is the test of love." Bishop Westcott

48. "In love, one always begins by deceiving oneself, and one always ends by deceiving others, and that is what the world calls romance." Oscar Wilde

RETIREMENT

Did you hear that the woman who gets cut in half at the circus retired? She retired in Pittsburgh and Cincinatti.

RICH

1. A man is a success if he can make more money than his wife can spend. A women is a success if she can find such a man.

2. A man is a success if he has a wife to tell him what to do and he has a secretary to do it.

3. A guy put a billboard up that read, "Old millionaire wants young woman." The next day he found one. Someone who wanted an older man with a big heart, but she said, "An enlarged heart would be even better."

4. I just want a man who is rich enough that when we go into Tiffany's he uses a shopping cart.

5. I want a guy that when he gets sick the IRS sends him get-well cards.

6. He's so rich that for Valentines Day he bought his wife Hallmark.

7. His wife got a craving for mints so he bought her Fort Knox.

8. He's so rich he has cattle branded with an unlisted number.

9. He's so rich he has a car with a prescription windshield.

10. He's so rich he has 3,000 head of cattle- in his freezer.

11. He says, "I'm not this tall, I'm sitting on my wallet."

12. I had a Texan in the other day that said, "My wife made a millionaire out of me." I asked him, "What were you before?" He said, "A multi-millionaire."

13. There was a blonde model that was married to a billionaire. When he died she had 3 days of mourning followed by several months of shopping.

14. I just want to be rich enough some day to pay off the national debt and repossess the United States.

15. Donald Trump once wanted to buy the United States, but the Japanese wouldn't sell.

16. I was so generous with my wife I had to marry her for my money.

17. His wife is so rich she has Gucci bags under her eyes.

RISK

A man decided to take his first skydive. He went through the training, and as he jumped from the plane he pulled the rip cord as he had been told to do. But nothing happened. Calmly applying his training, he reached for the emergency chute, and the cord came off in his hand. No parachute. Now panicked, he frantically tried to open the chute. That's when he noticed a man flying up from the earth towards him. He had no idea how the man was doing this, but he decided to take advantage of the opportunity. He shouted down to the approaching man, "Do you know anything about parachutes?" As they passed, the other man shouted back, "No! DO YOU KNOW ANYTHING ABOUT GAS STOVES?"

A lot of young people today are engaging in life-threatening sexual behavior without asking the important questions and have no answers when there are dire consequences.

ROMANCE

1. Did you know that man is the center of roMANce?

2. This woman attended a course called, "Fascinating Womanhood," so when she went home she decided to spice up her marriage. When her husband came home from work, she met him at the door dressed in nothing but Saran Wrap. He looked at her and said, "Just what I expected, leftovers again."

3. I knew a woman who wore a wig,, a wonder bra, and a butt booster, but said she was looking for a REAL man.

4. This farmer bought a prize bull. The next day his neighbor saw him putting a plow behind his bull. He said, "Joe, you just paid $10,000 for that prize bull, what are you doing?" He said, "Well, I just want to teach this bull the first lesson in life, that life's not all romance."

5. They have a new drug to make men grow breasts. Just what we need, a plumber with cleavage at both ends.

6. To have a successful relationship, everyone needs to LIE, CHEAT, STEAL, and DIVORCE.

A. You need to LIE in bed together a little longer (go to bed earlier and wake up later) and have more intimate moments with each other.

B. You need to CHEAT on your diet and take your mate out for a romantic meal at least once a week.

C. You need to STEAL some time away from your busy schedule and go on a romantic 72-hour weekend alone together and demonstrate how much you love each other.

D. You need to DIVORCE yourself from your many responsibilities and give more time to your relationships. Too often we major on the minors. We give much more time, money, energy, and effort to our jobs, and we just hope our relationships will somehow stay ecstatic by itself.

SELFISHNESS

"Selfishness is the root and source of all natural and moral evils." Nathaniel Emmons

SELLING SEX

1. "Many a man thinks he is buying pleasure, when he is really selling himself a slave to it." Benjamin Franklin

2. "A person who is going to commit an inhuman act, excuses himself by saying, 'I'm only human.'" Sydney Harris

3. Man is worse than an animal when he is an animal.

4. Promiscuous sex is the Hiroshima of love.

5. Promiscuous sex will get you as far as a cowboy who gets on his horse and rides in all directions at once.

SEX

1. Sex never ever made a good relationship, but a good relationship makes a great sex life, after marriage.

2. The greatest sex organ is on top of your shoulders.

3. The truth that most women don't realize is that the more you use sex to avoid losing a man, the greater the chance that you will lose him.

4. Sex is like fire, a dangerous servant and a fearful master.

5. Using sexuality wrong can turn a good thing into evil. Remember, Satan is a fallen angel.

6. In the act of loving, you arm another person against you.

7. "The physical union of the sexes only intensifies man's sense of solitude." Nicolas Berdyaev

8. The more one learns about sex, the less one knows.

9. "In efforts to soar above our nature, we invariably fall below it."   Edgar Allen Poe

10. "Man is a clever animal, who behaves like an imbecile."   Albert Schweitzer

11. Pleasure is more trouble than trouble.

12. Fire destroys that which feeds it.

13. "The weakness in human nature, goes by the name of strength".   Peter Ustinov

14. "Several excuses are always less convincing than one." Aldous Huxley

15. A meaningless phrase repeated again begins to resemble truth.

16. Proverbs 7:17-18   "I have perfumed my bed with myrrh, aloes, and cinnamon.   Come, let us take our fill of love until the morning."

Sex Statistics

1. When you rely on sex statistics, remember that research has recently proven that statistics are only accurate 68% of the time.

2. "If there is a 50-50 chance that something can go wrong, then nine times out of ten it will." Paul Harvey

3. Cookbooks still outsell sex books three to one.

Shy

1. I was so shy when I was a teenager I couldn't play tennis with a girl because I couldn't get myself to say "Love-30."

2. I wouldn't walk in a pet shop because I was afraid a parrot might try to strike up a conversation.

3. I was so shy I couldn't lead in silent prayer.

4. I was really shy; in fact, I was $20.00 too shy.

SHY CONT.

5. One shy guy was walking in the park with a girl. Suddenly he blurted out, "Will you marry me?" She said, "Why yes." He never said a word for three more hours as they just kept walking. Finally she said, "Well, aren't you going to say anything?" He said, "I think I already said too much."

6. When I was a teenager I dated a girl for 6 months, but she obviously didn't know it.

STRESS

One woman said to a psychiatrist, "You have to do something with my husband, he thinks he's a refrigerator." He said, "Why, that must be awfully hard on you." She said, "Oh, it is. He sleeps with his mouth open, and that little light keeps me awake."

TEMPTATION

1. "Every moment of resistance to temptation is a victory." Frederick Faber

2. "Too many teenagers can resist anything but temptation." Allen Unruh

THINKING AND SEX

1. "No question is so difficult to answer as that to which the answer is obvious." George Bernard Shaw

2. The finest bosom in nature is not so fine as imagination forms.

3. "Girls have an unfair advantage over men: if they can't get what they want by being smart, they can get it by being dumb." Yul Brynner

4. Science has discovered exactly where the thought processes occur, and in too many men it's below the belt.

5. Every man's battle: When the hormones say, yes, and the conscience says, no.

TIMES ARE CHANGING

1. One guy wanted to marry his horse, but the judge wouldn't let him because the horse wasn't 18.

2. In this day and age of frozen embryos one woman said, "I've got one in the oven, and two in the freezer."

3. Nowadays sex is getting more dangerous all the time. In fact, if a woman throws you a kiss you better duck.

TRUTH

The truth is more important than the consequences.

VIRTUE

1. "When we associate with the virtuous we form ourselves in imitation of their virtues, to at least lose, every day, something of our faults." Agapet

2. "There are some jobs where it is impossible for a man to be virtuous." Aristotle

3. "She's as pure as the driven slush." Allen Unruh

4. "It is easier to enrich ourselves with a thousand virtues, than to correct ourselves of a single fault." Jean De La Bruyere

5. "What is virtue? Reason in practice." J.J. De Chenier

6. "The more virtuous a man is, the less easily does he suspect others to be victorious." Cicero

7. "Virtue is its own reward." Cicero

8. "He that is good will infallibly become better, and he that is bad will as certainly become worse, for vice, virtue and time are three things that never stand still." Charles Caler Colton

9. "A large part of virtue consists of good habits." William Paley

10. "Virtue and a muscle are alike. If neither of these are exercised they get weak and flabby." Richard Rooney

11. "No virtue is safe that is not enthusiastic." John Seeley

VIRTUE CONT.

12. "Nature does not bestow virtue. To be good is an art." Seneca

13. "Few men have virtue to withstand the highest bidder." George Washington

14. "One should seek virtue for its own sake and not from hope or fear, or any external motive. It is in virtue that happiness consists, for virtue is the state of mind which tends to make the whole of life harmonious." Zeno of Citium

15. "Who can find a virtuous woman? For her price is far above rubies. The heart of her husband doth safely trust in her, so that he shall have no need of spoil. She will do him good and not evil all the days of her life." Proverbs 31:10-12

WEATHER

1. It got so cold in South Dakota one day that one bachelor said he almost got married.

2. It was so cold one night my wife slept with her fur coat on, and I kept dreaming of coyotes.

3. My wife is so cold, she froze the waterbed, and broke my arm on the ice.

4. Many are cold but few are frozen.

WIVES

1. Webster wrote the dictionary because of his wife. To everything he would say, she would ask, "What's that supposed to mean?"

2. When Abe Lincoln was asked, "Is it good to get married?" He answered, "Either way, you'll repent."

3. Socrates said, "If you marry a good wife, you'll lead a good life; if you marry a bad one, you'll become a philosopher."

4. One guy became a world champion sculptor with no arms. How did he do that? He held a chisel in his mouth while his wife hit him in the back of the head with a mallet.

5. This guy died and the pastor came to the funeral and said to his widow, "I'm so sorry Martha, about your husband, what were his last words?" She said, "You don't fool me one bit with that shotgun Martha, you couldn't hit the broadside of a barn."

6. Edison, after 10,000 experiments, finally got the light bulb to light up and he ran upstairs and said to his wife, "Look honey what I have here." She said, "Tommy, would you shut out that dang light and come to bed?"

7. Francis Scott Key's wife said after he wrote the Star Spangled Banner, "Honey, now why don't you write a song that people can sing sitting down."

8. My wife and I have an agreement: I don't try to run her life and I don't try to run mine.

9. My wife has the philosophy that I can do anything she sets her mind to.

10. Every man's dream is to someday live the lifestyle that his wife and kids do.

WIVES CONT.

11. One guy's wife was so cold she froze the waterbed. He broke his arm on the ice.

12. Ever since we got our waterbed, we've been drifting apart.

13. I grew up in a large family. In fact, I never slept alone until I got married.

14. When my wife and I got married, we vowed to grow old together. We just didn't realize it was going to be the first year.

15. One guy said to his wife, "I was a fool when I married you." She said, "I suppose you were, but I was so infatuated, I didn't notice at the time."

16. A husband and wife were driving down the road and she spotted a donkey in a pasture. She said to her husband, "Relatives of yours?" He looked and said, "Yes, honey, by marriage."

17. One woman said, "Some people think my husband's a pain in the neck, but I have a much lower opinion of him."

18. A guy wrote Billy Graham once and asked, "Are you married to the same woman in heaven? I got to know, I may be able to tolerate her on earth, but for eternity, I can't stand the thought."

19. My wife gave me loafers and leisure slacks for Christmas, and now she complains because I try to act the way I'm dressed.

20. If I ever lay on the couch, that immediately spurs my wife's brain into thinking of things I need to be doing. Clean out the garage, mow the lawn, etc.

21. One guy, after 6 hours of football, could hardly get out of the couch. His wife saidto him, "Is that what they call a tight end?"

22. One guy said, "Honey, I do not hate your relative; I like your mother-in-law a lot better than mine."

23. Never argue with a woman when she's tired or rested. And men should never miss a good chance to shut up.

24. There are two theories on how to argue with a woman, and neither of them work.

25. The secret to happiness in our marriage is that we both go out twice a week. I go Mondays and Thursdays and she goes Tuesdays and Fridays.

26. My wife and I kid each other a lot, but actually there's nothing I wouldn't do for her and there's nothing she wouldn't do for me. And that's the way it's been for years. We've done nothing for each other.

27. My wife dresses to kill. She cooks the same way. Where there's smoke, there she is, cooking. The roaches eat out at our house.

28. "Never go to bed angry. Stay up and fight!" Phyllis Diller

29. "When the candles are out, all women are fair." Plutarch

30. We never go to bed with wrath on our hearts towards each other. We haven't slept in weeks.

31. I worship the ground she walks on, especially the property she owns in Palm Springs.

32. When my wife was asked, "Do you take this man for richer or poorer?" she said, "For richer."

33. "The only difference between a successful marriage and a mediocre one consists of leaving about 3 or 4 things a day left unsaid." Harlan Miller

34. "When a guy brings his wife flowers for no reason, there's a reason." Molly McGee

35. "Many a man has fallen in love with a girl in a light so dim he would not have chosen a suit by it." Maurice Chevalier

36. "I haven't spoken to my wife in years. I don't want to interrupt her." Rodney Dangerfield

37. "My husband yells comments like, 'How long til you're ready?' I say, 'Throw out a date.'" Wendy Morgan

38. Keeping a secret from my wife is like trying to sneak daylight past a rooster.

39. Annoyed wife to husband: "Can't you just say we've been married 24 years instead of almost a quarter of a century?"

40. Research has recently revealed that there are more men in mental hospitals than women- which finally proves the old argument about who's driving who crazy.

41. There are a number a mechanical devices which increase sexual arousal, particularly in women. Chief among them is the Mercedes- Benz 380 SL convertible.

42. Even Solomon said to his 10,000 wives and concubines, "All right, which one of you doesn't have a headache."

43. My wife loves bird watching so I bought her a pair of binoculars and a bird.

44. Last night my wife slept with her fur coat on and I kept dreaming of coyotes.

45. My wife said, "Honey, I dreamed you gave me $100.00 last night; you wouldn't want to ruin my dream would you?" I said, "No, dear, you can keep the $100.00."

46. My wife watches everything I do with a fine tooth comb.

47. Wife: "Some people think my husband's a pain in the neck, but I've got a much lower opinion of him."

48. My wife makes all the small decisions like where we're going to live, what kind of house we live in, where we travel. I make the big decisions like, "Who's going to win the war in the Middle East?"

49. I call my wife Teddy Roosevelt for short. Every store she goes in she hollers "CHARGE!" She buys everything marked down. Last week she bought an escalator.

WOMEN

1. The weaker sex is actually the stronger sex because the weakness of the stronger sex is the weaker sex.

2. Any man who claims he can read a woman like a book must be a mystery fan.

3. Hell hath no fury like the lawyer of a woman scorned.

4. You don't know anything about a woman until you meet her in court.

5. There are two ways to make a woman happy. First, let her think she's having her way. And second, let her have it.

6. Never argue with a woman when she's tired or rested.

7. A man is never so weak as when a woman tells him how strong he is.

8. It takes a lot of experience for a girl to kiss like a beginner.

9. You can't make a silk purse out of a sows ear but many a woman has gotten a mink coat out of an old goat.

10. "The man who gets along best with women is the man who knows how to get along without them." Charles Baudelaire

11. "Most women set out to change a man, but when they change him, they don't like him." Marlene Dietrich

12. "Never play cards with a man called Doc. Never eat in a place called Mom's. Never sleep with a woman whose troubles are worse than your own." Nelson Algren

13. A youthful figure is what you get when you ask a woman her age. Anonymous

14. "It is the good girls that keep the diaries. The bad ones never have the time." Tallulah Bankhead

15. "The way to fight a woman is with your hat. Grab it and run." John Barrymore

16. "Most women are not so young as they're painted." Max Beerbohm

17. "Empty wine bottles have a bad opinion of women."
Ambrose Bierce

18. "Women would be more charming if one could fall into her arms without falling into her hands." Ambrose Bierce

19. "The trouble with most women is that they get all excited about nothing and then they marry him." Cher

20. "Being a woman is terribly difficult since it consists primarily in dealing with men." Joseph Conrad

21. "The average man is more interested in a woman who is interested in him than he is in a woman with beautiful legs." Marlene Dietrich

22. "It isn't that gentlemen really prefer blondes. It's just that we look dumber." Anita Loos

23. "If God had wanted us to think with our wombs, why did he give us a brain?" Claire Luce

24. There's a new birth control pill for men. And so far it's been extremely effective. Not one man has gotten pregnant.

25. "A kiss can be a comma, a question mark, or an exclamation point. That's basic spelling that every woman ought to know." Mistinguette

26. "I don't mind living in a man's world as long as I can be a woman in it." Marilyn Monroe

27. "If women didn't exist all the money in the world would have no meaning." Aristotle Onassis

28. "When the candles are out, all women are fair." Plutarch

29. "I never expected to see the day where women get sunburned the places they do now." Will Rogers

30. What can a man say to a woman in a thong? Pardon me mam but your rear end has swallowed up your bathing suit.

31. "From birth to age 18, a girl needs good parents, from 18 to 35 she needs good looks, from 35 to 55 she needs a good personality, and from 55 on she needs cash." Sophie Tucker

32. "Every man has a secret ambition. To outsmart horses, fish and women." Mark Twain

33. "My advice to girls: first, don't smoke - to excess; second, don't drink - to excess; third, don't marry - to excess." Mark Twain

34. Young women should keep their head up and their skirts down.

35. "I like a woman with a head on her shoulders, I hate necks." Steve Martin

36. Some women you couldn't warm up to if you were cremated with them.

37. A woman libber got on a crowded bus and a guy got up to give her his seat. She said, "You must not give up your seat, I insist." He said, "Insist all you want lady, this is the street I get off."

WOMEN CONT.

38. When women get depressed they go shopping. Men invade another country.

39. There are two theories on how to argue with a woman and neither of them work.

WOMEN'S LIB

1. If it weren't for Adam's rib, we'd never have had women's lib.

2. One women's libber started out a speech: "Where would you men be without us women?" A guy in the back shouted, "In the Garden of Eden."

3. One guy said, "I'm sure glad my wife joined women's lib, now she hates all men, not just me."

BY DR. ALLEN UNRUH

CONCLUSION

We all have to learn how to be effective fathers and husbands, mothers and wives. In fact, there's so much to learn that couples often feel overwhelmed. We've all been there. Do you sometimes feel you're not doing enough?

Let me simplify life for you. "Put on love." There it is. Love is everything your relationship needs. On love hangeth the whole law. It binds all virtues into one. It covers your family with the warm blanket of security. Your love, expressed daily, is the best gift you can give to your family and to each other.

You will continue to make mistakes. Your partner will ignore your budget. You understand that you both live with imperfect people. But when you offer self-giving love on a regular basis, imperfections are overlooked.

The fruits of the spirit (compassion, kindness, humility, gentleness, and patience), all wrapped up in the brightly colored paper of love, will do more to sustain your relationship than anything else.

We should do all we can to pursue excellence in our relationships. Life is a journey; it's not a destination. Affirm each other every day. Pray for a fresh infusion of love and for ways to practically express it to each other on a day to day basis. Form the habit of loving.

He who finds himself, shall lose himself.

Dr. Allen is a chiropractor. Since 1970, he has worked his fingers to the bone and lived on back pay.

Dr. Unruh was born in a one room shack in a one horse town. He went to a one room school house. He was a farm boy, and was outstanding in his field. He picked corn by hand and it went to his head.

He read the book, "The Power of One," and started studying one liners...because he can't remember two. Early on, he discovered the secret of how to make people laugh; he sure knows how to keep a secret! He has entertained literally DOZENS of people. He performed in front of 4 presidents — Mount Rushmore. Allen is great with words, not with jokes, but great with words. It takes years to be a great comedian, he just hasn't reached that year yet.

He has never won an Oscar, but he did win an Oscar Meier Wiener once. He says, "Comedy is not an easy job. First of all you have to stand up to do it." He's a man who knows where he is...most of the time. Dr. Unruh hopes comedy will bring him a steak in the future—he's getting tired of Chicken Ala King.

He crams 30 minutes of entertainment into 9. Most people who make the big time are great, great looking,and have personality and connections, but he's living proof that you don't need any of those things. As his wife puts it, "I always know what is on his mind...NOTHING!"

Dr. Allen D. Unruh
600 N. Western Avenue
Sioux Falls, SD 57104
605-332-1962
605-332-5931 (fax)
email: adunruh@drunruh.com

Dr. Allen Unruh is a Chiropractic Physician, in active practice since 1970. He and his wife, Leslee, have five grown children and four grandchildren. Leslee is the founder of the National Abstinence Clearinghouse.

Dr. Unruh is the author of six other books including:

So You Think Your Job's Bad

Romance 101

Father Power

Adversity

My Favorite Quotes

If The Government Doesn't Get Off Our Backs The Whole Country Will Need A Chiropractor

Dr. Unruh has always used humor to communicate life's most important lessons. For information or to have Dr. Unruh speak to your organization please call:

1-800-399-5158

"Dr. Allen Unruh is one of the most humorous guys that I know, he is the king of one-liners! He could best be described as a dispenser of and believer in, good, clean humor."

Dan Carlson, Faith Baptist Fellowship

South Dakota's only Clean Comedian! *"Allen Unruh makes me laugh! He has SO much great material. I love the way he can customize his comedy routine to fit an audience of any age or background."*

Adam Christing, President, National Clean Comedians